PORN-FREE
IN
40 DAYS

Mark Denison, D.Min.

Author of

Porn in the Pew
365 Days to Sexual Integrity
90-Day Recovery Guide

AUSTIN
BROTHERS PUBLISHING

Fort Worth TX 76137

www.abpbooks.com

Porn-Free in 40 Days

© Mark Denison 2019

ISBN: 978-1-7324846-6-5

Printed in the United States of America

2019—First Edition

*I dedicate this work to all who seek
the joy of a porn-free life.*

Table of Contents

PREFACE

You are to be congratulated for taking the first steps to recovery from porn addiction. If you commit the next 40 days to learning and applying specific tools for recovery, you will be a different person in 40 days from what you are today. These principles are making a difference in the lives of men all over the world – who are courageous enough to go all in. Here are just a few examples.

1. "Bill" – He had tried counseling, church, books, self-discipline, and personal retreats. But it was the principles contained in this simple guide that made the difference. Until 2017, Bill had never experienced one month of sobriety in his life. As of this writing, he has over one year. *And another thing – Bill is 93 years old.*

2. "Chip" – A seminary student committed to the ministry, Chip didn't know what it was to be free. He had prayed, read the Bible, and repented hundreds of times. But finally, after applying the tools in this guide, Chip is walking in freedom. *And another thing – Chip just got engaged.*

3. "Aaron" – A huge success in his field, Aaron had tried everything. But nothing seemed to work. Finally, he applied the principles in this 40-day guide and began working this plan. What had escaped him for 45 years is finally his – lasting sobriety and healthy recovery. *And another thing – Aaron is a licensed professional counselor.*

What has worked for others will work for you – if you go all in.

INTRODUCTION

Before you start Day 1, let me give you a quick off-ramp. This 40-day guide will only work if you pass the entrance exam. It begins with five "Thou shalt nots" and continues with the four things you must do in order to find real recovery.

Thou Shalt Not . . .

1. **Thou shalt not *minimize*.** If you go into this thinking your porn use is no big deal, everyone does it, and you can just cut back and be okay, you're done. Ask for your money back. This will do you no good. Because here's the deal – you are in for the fight of your life.

2. **Thou shalt not *mischaracterize*.** If you tell yourself, "I watch porn a few times every week, but it's not an addiction," and you believe it, you have a fool for an audience. You have an addiction, or you would have stopped already. And even if you don't have an addiction, it's better to overreact than underreact.

3. **Thou shalt not *spiritualize*.** Yes, you have a spiritual disconnect, a spiritual problem. But it is not just a spiritual problem.

It's okay to blame this on a demon, as long as you recognize that demon is you. Do you need to read the Bible more, go to church, and pray daily? Yes, but that only gets you to the starting line, not the finish line.

4. **Thou shalt not *sterilize*.** This isn't for wimps. You have to be willing to enter a world of dark secrets, get real, and face the music. Sugar coating it does no good. Dressing up your problem with more palatable language is like calling quick sand something less while you sink to your death.

5. **Thou shalt not *moralize*.** It's too easy to say, "If I was only a better person, I'd stop doing this." I have yet to meet the man or woman who said, "You know what, I'm just a bad person who wants to wreck his life and destroy everyone around him."

Thou Shalt . . .

1. **Be desperate.** You must come to hate your disease more than you love the feeling of the moment. You must learn to chase what you want most by denying what you want now. You must be all in, hungry, thirsty, willing to go to any length necessary, try things you've never considered before, and follow the directions of those who know a lot more about recovery than you do.

2. **Surrender to God.** You can't get around this one. You might say, "Well, I'm not a spiritual person." My response: "You aren't a sober person, either." The tools in this guide will help you find your way spiritually. But it only works if you are willing to surrender everything to God. He is in your corner. He will fight for you. But you have to trust him.

3. **Commit to community**. You cannot do this alone. You need others. This will probably mean going to 12-step meetings. It may mean joining some other recovery group. It will call for personal accountability. This is not natural, but it is necessary. I have years of recovery and total sobriety. But I still attend two 12-step meetings every week, have a sponsor, and sponsor others. Why? Because I need community. So do you.

4. **Be known**. This means disclosing to God, your spouse (if you are married), those you have hurt, and others. What do you disclose? To some – everything. This addiction thrives in secrecy. There are some in your life who don't need to know anything. Others need to know something. And someone needs to know everything. Until you are fully known you cannot be truly loved.

Let's Get Started . . .

Did you pass the test? Are you willing to not minimize, mischaracterize, spiritualize, sterilize, or moralize? Are you ready to embrace desperation, surrender, community, and disclosure? If so, you are in for a rewarding 40 days. This is not for the faint of heart. But if you are ready to lay down your porn and walk in freedom, you are on the right path.

Freedom is just around the corner . . .

Day 1
Own It!

Luke 15:17-20 *"When he came to his senses, he said . . . 'I will set out and go back to my father and say to him: Father, I have sinned against heaven and against you. I am no longer worthy to be called your son; make me like one of your hired servants.' So he got up and went to his father."*

Until you take ownership of your disease, you will not take responsibility for your recovery. The story of the prodigal son is a shining example of the magic of owning one's condition.

The younger brother traded what every addict does – he traded what he wanted *most* for what he wanted *now*. Had he waited until the appropriate time, he would have inherited a larger portion of his father's estate – with its accrued value. The man spent all he had on "wild living" (15:13). Then, after "he had spent everything," he hit bottom. And only then did he take ownership for his condition.

Finally, the prodigal "came to his senses" (15:17) and resolved to return home. He quit the blame game, owned his condition, and found redemption in the open arms of his loving father (15:21-24).

Does any of this sound familiar? Your porn addiction started small. But an innocent glance here and a quick look there soon snowballed out of control. You went from casual porn to "wild living."

Now you have a binary choice. You can continue to blame everyone else for your problem. Or you can own it. And until you own it, you won't beat it. The day you take responsibility for your porn habit is the day you will start down the long road of recovery. This can be that day.

Three Lessons

1. Until you take ownership of your disease, you will not take responsibility for your recovery.

2. You must trade what you want now for what you want most.

3. You have a binary choice. You can continue to blame others or you can own it. But you can't do both.

Today's Exercise

1. Write the name of the one person who must own your porn habit now: _____

2. If you wrote any name other than your own in the previous blank, correct it now!

3. If you are willing to take 100% responsibility for your addiction, and if you are ready to do something about it, sign your name and today's date.
   a. Name: _____
   b. Date: _____

4. Congratulate yourself for completing Day 1 of your 40 Days to Porn-Free Living!

Day 2

Desperate

2 Kings 5:15 *"Naaman went down and dipped himself in the Jordan seven times, as the man of God had told him, and his flesh was restored and became clean like that of a young boy."*

Hippocrates said it first: "Desperate times call for desperate measures." For a man named Naaman, it was time for desperate measures.

Naaman was the commander of the army of Aram. The Bible says he was a valiant soldier, but he had one problem – he was a leper. This horrific disease would render him a hopeless, hapless, homeless vagrant. Suddenly, in his grief he found religion.

Naaman sent for the local preacher, a prophet by the name of Elisha. "What do I do?" he asked. Elisha offered one way out, but it would mean doing something the commander would find embarrassing and senseless.

"Go wash yourself seven times in the Jordan," he was told (5:10). Naaman resisted, and only became worse. Eventually, when absolute desperation kicked in, he did the unexpected. He dipped himself in the muddy waters seven times. And his healing began.

You know you have a problem, or you wouldn't be reading this right now. But the real question is this – Are you desperate? Are you willing to go to any measures necessary to overcome your porn addiction?

To get well, like Naaman, you will have to do some things that may not make sense at first, such as going to therapy, attending a 12-step group, getting a sponsor, working the 12 steps, and admitting out loud, "My name is _____, and I am a sex addict."

Four Lessons

1. Only when you become desperate will you get well.

2. In order to get where you want to be you will have to do things you don't want to do.

3. Recovery is not comfortable.

4. Until you embrace a new strategy you will not have new results.

Today's Exercise

1. Which of the following steps are you willing to take, in order to overcome your porn habit?

   a. Therapy _____
   b. Attend Celebrate Recovery _____
   c. Attend Sexaholics Anonymous _____
   d. Read daily recovery devotions _____
   e. Pray daily _____
   f. Confess your struggle to your spouse _____
   g. Purchase accountability software _____
   h. Get a sponsor _____

2. How much time are you willing to set aside each day to do the necessary work for genuine recovery? _____

3. List three things you will do this week, even though they may not make sense or come easily.

   a. _____
   b. _____
   c. _____

Day 3

Complete Surrender

John 5:8-9 *"Jesus said to him, 'Get up! Pick up your mat and walk.' At once the man was healed; he picked up his mat and walked."*

One day, on his way to a Jewish festival, Jesus came upon several beggars beside a small body of water. His eye was drawn to a particular man, a paralytic of 38 years. Jesus asked him an unusual question: "Do you want to get well?" (5:6).

When the man said he did, he was told to play the part of the fool. "Pick up your mat and walk," Jesus said (5:8). It was in that moment – when the man did the improbable – that Jesus did the impossible. It was when the man surrendered, by doing what Jesus had commanded, that he was made well.

Nothing matters more to recovery than surrender. Why? Because it is when you step down that God steps up. Andrew Murray said it like this: "God is ready to assume full responsibility for the life wholly yielded to him."

In 12-step work, many get stuck on Step 3 – "Made a decision to turn my life and my will over to the care of God as I understood him." Surrender doesn't come easily.

You must understand, surrender is not passive. There is an old saying, "If five frogs sat on a log and four decided to jump off, the number remaining on the log was five." Deciding to jump is not jumping. Deciding to surrender is not surrender. If you are to overcome your porn addiction, you will have to decide to surrender everything to God. But then you must actually surrender everything to God.

Four Lessons

1. It is when you step down that God steps up.

2. God is ready to assume full responsibility for the life wholly yielded to him.

3. It is when you get under the One who is to be over you that you can get over that which is to be under you.

4. It is when you do the improbable that God does the impossible.

Today's Exercise

1. Are you willing to surrender your life and will to God right now?

    a. Yes _____
    b. No _____

2. Pray this prayer, taken from the Third Step of Alcoholics Anonymous:

> *"God, I offer myself to you to build with me and do with me as you will. Relieve me of the bondage of self, that I may better do your will. Take away my difficulties, that victory over them may bear witness to those I would help of your power, your love, and your way of life."*

Day 4
Define Sobriety

Luke 14:28-30 *"Suppose one of you wants to build a tower. Won't you first sit down and estimate the cost to see if you have enough money to complete it? For if you lay the foundation and are not able to finish it, everyone who sees it will ridicule you, saying, 'This person began to build and wasn't able to finish.'"*

Jesus taught his followers that in order to achieve anything in life, we must first count the cost. He offered two examples: (a) a man building a tower, and (b) a king going to war. In each instance, it was critical to define the cost of victory.

Recovery is a process of building. And it is war. You will build upon the work of each previous day, and you will be at war with spiritual powers, your own past, and daily temptations. But the building can be completed and the war can be won.

The building you seek to erect is called sobriety. Matthew Perry said it well: "If I don't have sobriety, I don't have anything." But what does it mean to be sober?

The DSM manual, the standard criteria for the field of psychiatry, never designates abstinence as a precedent for sobriety. But the Sexaholics Anonymous "white book" provides an excellent definition of sexual sobriety. "For the sexaholic, any form of sex with one's self or with partners other than the spouse is progressively addictive and destructive" (page 1). Going even further, the book reads, "Lust is the driving force behind our sexual acting out, and true sobriety includes progressive victory over lust" (page 4).

Sobriety is a state (not acting out) as well as a goal (progressive victory over lust).

Five Lessons

1. You cannot achieve your goal until you define it.

2. Sobriety is both a state (not acting out) and a goal (progressive victory over lust).

3. If you don't have sobriety, you don't have anything.

4. If you aren't all in with your recovery, you aren't in at all.

5. If you allow yourself a "little porn" or a "little masturbation," you will never be well.

Today's Exercise

Write your definition of sobriety: _____

_____

_____

_____

_____

_____

_____

Day 5

God's #1 Rule

Matthew 9:9 *"As Jesus went on from there, he saw a man named Matthew sitting at the tax collector's booth. 'Follow me,' he told him, and Matthew got up and followed him."*

Every day, employees at a delivery business loading dock were greeted by the same sign hanging on the wall:

Ten Rules

Rule 1: Deliver the goods.
Rules 2-10: Obey the first rule.

Jesus had had a busy day. He healed a paralyzed man, forgave a man's sins, sparred with religious leaders, and spoke to a large crowd. Then, as Jesus moved away from the crowd, he walked by the most unpopular man in town. His name was Matthew and he was a tax collector. In those days, tax collectors literally robbed the people blind, in the name of the Roman government.

There are a lot of things Jesus could have said to the man. "Stop doing what you're doing, then follow me." "Apologize to those you have hurt, then follow me." "Make amends, then follow me." "Get in therapy, then follow me."

Nope. Jesus kept it simple. He only said, "Follow me." Why? Because that is the #1 rule for getting well.

It is good to seek therapy, join a group, and dig into your past. Learn your family history and confront the trauma of your past. (We all have some.) But until you get the #1 rule right, the others don't matter.

Do what Matthew did. Follow Jesus.

Four Lessons

1. Religion has a lot of rules. Jesus had one – "Come, follow me."

2. The Christian life is not about rules. It's about relationship.

3. You can't break your porn habit, and then follow Jesus. But you can follow Jesus, and then break your porn habit.

4. You can only follow Jesus when you hear him calling. You're hearing him right now, so what are you waiting for?

Today's Exercise

Are you already a Christ-follower? _____

Are you ready to become a Christ-follower now? _____

If you answered "yes" to the last question, express to God your desire to follow him. Pray something like this:

> *"Dear God, I cannot beat this porn addiction on my own. I know, because I've tried to for years. I recognize my need for you in my life and by my side. So, the best I know how, I commit my life to the same Jesus who told Matthew to follow him. I openly and freely ask for your forgiveness of all the things I have done and the pain I have caused. I trust you as my Lord, my Savior, my everything. I commit to following you from this day forward."*

Day 6

An Honest Inventory

Luke 19:8 *"Zacchaeus stood up and said to the Lord, 'Look, Lord! Here and now I give half of my possessions to the poor, and if I have cheated anybody out of anything, I will pay back four times the amount.'"*

We all know the story of Zacchaeus. Being vertically challenged, he couldn't see Jesus as he passed through the streets of Jericho - until he climbed up in a sycamore tree. Jesus looked up and Zacchaeus came down. He then welcomed Jesus into his home.

That's when real life change took place. Zacchaeus was so committed to a new way of life that he offered - without any prompting from Jesus - to pay back all the clients he had swindled through the years as a tax collector.

Zacchaeus went even further, offering to pay them 400 percent of what he had taken. Think about that. Zacchaeus was willing to not only make restitution, but to do an accounting of the pain he had caused. Only by doing a thorough audit of his financial dealings was this even possible.

If you are to progress in your battle with pornography, you will need to do an honest inventory of what you have done and the pain you have caused.

This is where it will be clear as to whether or not you are serious about your recovery. Mahatma Gandhi said, "To believe in something and not live it is dishonest."

If you are to be successful in your recovery, you must get honest. Then you must complete an inventory of the effects of what you have done.

Four Lessons

1. Before you can become clean, you have to come clean.

2. The degree to which you are serious about recovery will be measured by the length to which you are willing to go to make things right with those whom you have hurt.

3. To believe something is admirable. But to not live what you believe is dishonest.

4. Successful recovery requires an audit of what you have done.

Today's Exercise

Estimate the number of hours you have spent watching porn:

_____

Estimate the amount you have spent on porn: $_____

Write the names of a few people your porn use has harmed:

    a. _____

    b. _____

    c. _____

    d. _____

    e. _____

Commit to making amends to each person on your list.

Day 7

Custody of Your Eyes

Genesis 19:24-26 *"The Lord rained down burning sulfur on Sodom and Gomorrah. But Lot's wife looked back, and she became a pillar of salt."*

Sin comes at a price. Because the cities of Sodom and Gomorrah had not relented in their sexual debauchery, God warned of pending judgment. But he offered his servant Lot a warning the night before. The angels told Lot, "Hurry! Take your wife and your two daughters who are here, or you will be swept away when the city is punished" (19:15).

God gave further instructions. "Flee for your lives! Don't look back, and don't stop anywhere in the plain! Flee to the mountains or you will be swept away!" (19:17).

But we read, "Lot's wife looked back, and she became a pillar of salt" (19:26).

She looked back when she should have been looking forward. And in an instant, Lot's wife became an example for us all. When we fail to take custody of our eyes and when we let a quick glance become a stare, we are on the verge of real trouble.

Whatever captures your eye today will own your heart tomorrow. That's why it is so important to watch what you watch.

What you take in through your eyes will stay with you for years. Most guys can't remember what they had for breakfast today, but the image of a certain woman, picture, or video remains fixed in their head decades later. The best solution on how to deal with sensual images is to avoid them in the first place.

You know where to find porn. It's all over your past. But learn the lesson that cost Lot's wife her life. Don't look back!

Four Lessons

1. Whatever captures your eye today will own your heart tomorrow.

2. Don't look back when you should be looking ahead.

3. When a glance becomes a stare, you're in trouble.

4. The best solution for dealing with sensual images is to avoid them in the first place.

Today's Exercise

1. Will you commit to not looking at sensual images?

    a. Yes _____
    b. No _____

2. List some ways to avoid seeing the kind of women or images that bring you the most temptations:

    a. _____
    b. _____
    c. _____
    d. _____
    e. _____

Day 8

Trash the Stash

Deuteronomy 7:25-26 *"The images of their gods you are to burn in the fire. Do not covet the silver and gold on them, and do not take it for yourselves, or you will be ensnared by it, for it is detestable to the Lord your God. Do not bring a detestable thing into your house."*

When God told Moses to drive the enemies from their land – the Hittites, Girgashites, Amorites, Canaanites, and Jebusites – he warned against compromise on any level. "Do not make a treaty with them," he said (7:2). He continued, "Do not give your daughters to their sons" (7:3).

God told his children to not take in the gold or silver from their defeated foes, nor to embrace any of their other possessions. He said to not even bring these things into their house (7:26).

What have you brought into your house? Pornographic magazines? Lingerie ads? Women's clothing catalogues? Or maybe it's not what you brought into your house, but what was already there – on your computer.

We live in a day when 98 percent of men have viewed pornography and 62 percent of the men in church are looking at porn at least once a month. They do it at the office, at home, or anywhere else that is convenient.

The answer is clear: Trash the stash! It's time to take out your garbage before your garbage takes you out. Do an analysis of your computer, your desk drawer, etc. Wherever you've hidden your stash, it's time to take out the trash.

Four Lessons

1. You can take out your garbage. Or your garbage will take you out.

2. You are not what you portray. You are what you hide.

3. You must get rid of every hint of pornography before it destroys your life.

4. Sexual addiction is progressive. Unless you deal with it immediately, your porn habit will only get worse.

Today's Exercise

1. Make a list of all the places where you have stashed your porn. Include electronic devices as well as physical places.

    a. Electronic devices:
        1) _____
        2) _____
        3) _____
        4) _____
    b. Physical places:
        1) _____
        2) _____
        3) _____
        4) _____

2. Throw it all out. Wipe it clean. Take out the trash – today.

Day 9
Life Recovery Bible

Joshua 1:8 *"Keep this Book of the Law always on your lips; meditate on it day and night, so that you may be careful to do everything written in it. Then you will be prosperous and successful."*

Joshua was tasked with getting the ball over the goal line. Moses had been a tremendous leader. But it was Joshua who was commissioned with the job of leading God's children into the Holy Land. This would be an achievement of unimaginable proportions.

How would Joshua find success? God did not offer a military strategy or a lesson on leadership. He said to meditate on the Word. Do this, God said, and "you will be prosperous and successful" (1:8).

You need to read recovery materials. (I recommend my books on addiction recovery.) But mostly, you need to read and meditate on God's Word.

Alexander Graham Bell said, "Consecrate your thoughts upon the work at hand. The sun's rays do not burn until brought to a focus."

Nothing brings things into focus like God's Word. Practice the three 'L's: (a) love the Word, (b) learn the Word, and (c) live the Word. Getting into the Word is a daily habit that feeds recovery like nothing else.

Three Lessons

1. To find success, you need to be in the Word every day.

2. When you read the Bible, do so with one question in mind: "How does this help my recovery?"

3. What God does *through* you tomorrow will depend on what you let him do *in* you today.

Today's Exercise

1. Will you commit to daily Bible reading? _____

2. There is a wonderful resource for those in recovery. It's the Life Recovery Bible. The LRB is full of devotions and amazing commentary for application to those who suffer from any addiction. Our ministry believes in the LRB so much that we give it away to anyone who asks. If you do not already have a Life Recovery Bible, contact our ministry today, and we will ship you one this week. No cost for the Bible. Free shipping. Contact us today at TheresStillHope.org.

Day 10
Knock Three Times

Mark 1:35 *"Very early in the morning, while it was still dark, Jesus got up, left the house and went off to a solitary place, where he prayed."*

What we do in the morning matters. What mattered to Jesus? It's pretty clear. Early in his ministry - he wasn't out of the first chapter of Mark yet - we read that Jesus got up well before dawn, left the place where he was staying, and got alone to pray. Jesus didn't pray because he didn't have much going on in his life, but because he did.

If you could have overcome your porn problem in your own power, you already would have. You need to tap into your Higher Power. There is no better way to do that than through prayer.

Charles Spurgeon called prayer "a spiritual transaction with the Creator of Heaven and Earth." Oswald Chambers wrote, "It's not so much that prayer changes things, but that prayer changes me."

No one asks for a porn addiction. What we take in through our eyes takes over without waiting for the slightest invitation. The porn addict becomes like the boy possessed by a demon. Jesus said the demon could be cast out, but "this kind can come out only by prayer" (Mark 9:29).

If you are tired of battling the demons, it's time to pray. If you have sought freedom in your own strength, it's time to pray. If you have tried therapy, 12 steps, and reading a pile of materials, but still come up short - it's time to pray.

Three Lessons

1. If you could have overcome your struggle in your own power, you already would have by now.

2. It's not so much that prayer changes things. Prayer changes you.

3. You can do much after you pray, but very little until you pray.

Today's Exercise

1. There's an old song that says to "knock three times on the ceiling if you want me." If you want to connect with the One upstairs, try knocking three times - each day.

2. Try praying according to the ACTS formula. Write down one specific, short prayer in each of these four categories, then take a few minutes to pray for each:

   a. Adoration: _____

   _____

   b. Confession: _____

   _____

   c. Thanksgiving: _____

   _____

   d. Supplication: _____

   _____

Day 11

Forgive Yourself

Matthew 26:74-75 *"Then Peter denied Jesus a third time, and he swore to them, 'I don't know the man!' Immediately a rooster crowed. Then Peter remembered the word Jesus had spoken: 'Before the rooster crows, you will disown me three times.' And he went outside and wept bitterly."*

Jesus warned Peter that he would fall. Peter was adamant in his denial. "Even if all fall away, I never will" (26:33). And then he did. But what defined Peter was not what he did, but how he responded. He wept bitterly. This was an expression of remorse.

Peter was broken by his sin. Then grace stepped in. The God of the second chance picked Peter up, dusted him off, and propped him back up – just in time to preach the most significant sermon since the resurrection. You can read about it in Acts 2.

Peter disappointed God – and himself. The road to recovery was based on forgiveness from God – and himself.

To overcome your porn addiction, you have to learn to forgive yourself. Have you messed up? Absolutely! But for every sin there is forgiveness, for every slip there is grace, and for every relapse there is mercy.

You really have only two choices: forgiveness and resentment. M.L. Stedman wrote, in *The Light Between Oceans*, "You only have to forgive once. To resent, you have to do it all day, every day."

Are you ready to move forward in your recovery? Are you ready to take the next step? Then learn the art of forgiveness. Start with yourself.

Four Lessons

1. The road to recovery is paved with forgiveness – from God and yourself.

2. For every sin there is forgiveness, for every slip there is grace, and for every relapse there is mercy.

3. To overcome your porn addiction, you have to learn to forgive yourself.

4. You cannot forgive others until you learn to forgive yourself.

Today's Exercise

1. You can practice resentment or forgiveness. Pick one.

2. Take five minutes to talk to yourself and to God.

    a. Ask God for his forgiveness for your porn habit.

    b. Forgive yourself. Tell yourself the things you are letting go of, then release yourself from the guilt and shame; then release it and move on.

Day 12

Train the Brain

Luke 22:4, 47 *"Judas went to the chief priests and the officers of the temple guard and discussed with them how he might betray Jesus. While Jesus was speaking a crowd came up, and the man who was called Judas was leading them. He approached Jesus to betray him."*

What Judas thought, he eventually did. He only betrayed Jesus after the prayer on the Mount of Olives because it was in his head before then.

There is a common feeling that it is a certain body part that gets most men in trouble. I want to explode that myth. The fact is, the largest sex organ in every man is actually his brain.

Marcus Aurelius said, "The happiness of your life depends upon the quality of your thoughts; therefore, guard accordingly, and take care that you entertain no notions unsuitable to virtue and reasonable nature."

For those who struggle with pornography, there is this thing called euphoric recall. George Collins explains, "Euphoric recall is a function of your mind and your memory." Euphoric recall is the brain's way of revisiting a past sexual experience, to bring it to the front of our thinking, and even stimulate us to act out.

What is the answer? When past images and experiences invade your brain, shift to the present. Focus on something current, such as your faith or family. When these invasive thoughts take up residency in your mind, make sure they rent and do not own. Evict those thoughts before they have time to unpack their endless images into your head.

Five Lessons

1. Your biggest sex organ is your brain.

2. The happiness of your life depends on the quality of your thoughts.

3. Recovery doesn't begin with right actions; it ends there.

4. Lustful thoughts have your number, and they make calls when you least expect it. When you answer the call, it costs you – mightily.

5. Invasive thoughts are a part of recovery. It's what you do with those thoughts that matters.

Today's Exercise

1. Commit your thought life to God right now.

2. Write four ways you will divert your next invasive thoughts:

    a. _____

    b. _____

    c. _____

    d. _____

Day 13

Toxic Relationships

Genesis 39:11-12 *"One day Joseph went into the house to attend to his duties, and none of the household servants was inside. Potiphar's wife caught him by his cloak and said, 'Come to bed with me!' But he left his cloak in her hand and ran out of the house."*

The story of Joseph is a template for how we should all respond to sexual temptations. Joseph was taken captive in Egypt, but quickly found favor with the captain of Pharaoh's guard, a man named Potiphar. Potiphar put Joseph in charge of his estate. The Bible records, "Now Joseph was well-built and handsome, and after a while his master's wife took notice of him and said, 'Come to bed with me!'" (39:6-8).

The woman persisted "day after day" (39:10). Then, when she came onto Joseph one last time, he ran out of the house (39:12).

Doing the right thing came with a price. First, it meant self-denial, as Joseph denied the desires of his flesh. Second, it cost him a prison term, as Potiphar's wife accused him of a sexual advance.

But cutting off toxic relationships is always the wise thing to do. For Joseph, it meant finding God's favor in prison, and emerging stronger than ever. For you, when you cut off relationships with acting out partners or anyone else who feeds your addiction, you will soon find a freedom and peace you never knew.

Three Lessons

1. Cutting off toxic relationships is always the wise thing to do.

2. One of the chief determinants of your recovery will be the people you choose to spend time with.

3. You need to end every contact with former sex partners or old romantic interests other than your spouse.

Today's Exercise

1. Write the names of former acting out partners you need to cut out of your life:

    a. _____

    b. _____

    c. _____

    d. _____

    e. _____

2. Write the names of people in your life from whom you need to distance yourself, as they have become toxic:

    a. _____

    b. _____

    c. _____

    d. _____

    e. _____

Day 14

Move from Sodom

Genesis 13:12-13 *"Abram lived in the land of Canaan, while Lot lived among the cities of the plain and pitched his tents near Sodom. Now the people of Sodom were wicked and were sinning greatly against the Lord."*

As Abram's (soon to be known as Abraham) family expanded, it became necessary for them to split up and settle in two different lands. Abram gave the option to his relative Lot. He could settle where he wanted to, and Abram would go in a different direction.

Lot set out to the east, and he eventually settled in the shadows of the wicked city of Sodom. Notice, he didn't settle in Sodom, but rather near Sodom. One translation says he settled toward Sodom.

We know from our reading on Day 7 that the blatant sexual sins of Sodom would lead to their destruction. History tells us that the city was already well on its downward spiral when Lot settled nearby.

Notice what Lot did. He wanted to have it both ways. He wasn't about to move his family into Sodom. But he wanted to settle on the plains below, where he could see the city whenever he wanted.

The rest of the story was predictable. Six chapters later (Genesis 19), Lot had gone from *near* Sodom to *in* Sodom, and it would cost him the life of his wife.

That is how sexual sin always progresses. I'm sure you never intended to find yourself in the snares of pornography. You were just curious at first. Then a glance became a habit, which became a lifestyle. The solution? It's time to move as far away from Sodom as you can get.

Three Lessons

1. Where you visit today is where you will live tomorrow.

2. Porn use is always progressive.

3. You become what you tolerate.

Today's Exercise

1. What does Sodom represent in your life today? _____
   _____

2. What steps will you take to avoid Sodom?
   a. _____
   b. _____
   c. _____

Day 15
Close the Window

1 Kings 19:3-4 *"Elijah ran for his life. When he came to Beersheba in Judah, he left his servant there, while he himself went a day's journey into the wilderness. He came to a broom bush, sat down under it and prayed that he might die. 'I've had enough, Lord,' he said. 'Take my life; I am no better than my ancestors.'"*

In a period of a couple of chapters, Elijah prayed a boy back to life and called fire down from heaven. But then he let his guard down. The prophet who had just stared down 400 men was now afraid of one woman - Jezebel. She threatened Elijah, so he "ran for his life" (19:3).

Elijah did several things wrong. First, he ran from his problems rather than confront them. Second, he travelled alone. Third, he didn't take care of himself physically. (He did not eat.) Fourth, he overstated his dilemma. (He said he had no one else in his life.)

Elijah's big mistake was that he allowed negative thinking to enter his life.

Ben Franklin died on April 17, 1790, from sitting in front of an open window. The 84-year-old inventor had written, "I rise every morning and sit near the window in my chamber without any clothes, regardless of the season."

Because he left his window open, Ben Franklin eventually contracted pneumonia and died. That is a parable on addiction. Just as Elijah opened his "window" to negative thinking and Ben Franklin opened his window to the outside elements, a porn addict has opened the window of his computer, a relationship at work, or some other temptation.

Three Lessons

1. Today's victory is no guarantee of tomorrow's success.

2. You cannot afford to open yourself up to unnecessary temptations.

3. The window opens and closes from the inside.

Today's Exercise

1. What are the temptations that can torpedo your recovery if you are not diligent?

   a. _____

   b. _____

   c. _____

   d. _____

2. What steps will you take today to close your window?

   a. _____

   b. _____

   c. _____

   d. _____

Day 16

No More Secrets

Acts 5:1-3 *"Now a man named Ananias, together with his wife Sapphira, sold a piece of property. With his wife's full knowledge he kept back part of the money for himself, but brought the rest and put it at the apostles' feet. Then Peter said, 'Ananias, how is it that Satan has so filled your heart that you have lied to the Holy Spirit and have kept for yourself some of the money you received for the land?'"*

Secrets kill.

There is no better example in Scripture than that of Ananias and Sapphira. They did a very good deed by selling a piece of real estate and giving some of the profits to the Lord's work. But that's where the story went south.

Ananias and Sapphira had apparently led Peter to believe their gift represented 100 percent of the land sale. But they held some of the money back, to use on themselves. The problem wasn't that they kept some of the money, but that they lied about it.

Secrets kill.

Peter called Ananias out for his deception. He said, "You have not lied just to human beings, but to God" (5:4). Then we read, "When Ananias heard this, he fell down and died" (5:5).

Secrets kill.

Someone needs to know your deepest secrets. Not everyone – but someone. Why? Because secrecy is the incubator of addiction. As counterintuitive as it may sound, your biggest threat to recovery is not your repeated use of porn; it is your reluctance to tell somebody.

Five Lessons

1. A man is crippled by his guilt and buried by his secrets.

2. You aren't what you think you are. You are what you hide.

3. Secrecy is the incubator of addiction.

4. God doesn't judge you by what you give, but by what you hold onto.

5. Expose your secrets, or your secrets will expose you.

Today's Exercise

1. What secret are you holding onto, that nobody else knows about? _____

2. With whom will you share this secret? _____
_____

Day 17

Community

Acts 2:42, 44, 46 *"They devoted themselves to the apostles' teaching and fellowship . . . All the believers were together and had everything in common . . . Every day they continued to meet together in the temple courts. They broke bread in their homes and ate together with glad and sincere hearts."*

Recovery is a team sport. When Legion came to faith, Jesus told him to go home and tell his friends (Mark 5). When the paralytic was healed, he was found in church the next day (John 5). And when the disciples gathered to hear Peter's great sermon of Pentecost, their commitment to community was unmistakable.

Notice some of the words used to describe their community: "fellowship, breaking of bread, prayers, together, had all things in common, gave to all men as they had need, continued daily, one accord."

Michael Leahy, founder of BraveHearts, contends, "Only one in ten thousand get well without the help of others."

Isolation is the enemy of recovery. You need others in your life. Follow the example of Jesus, who had his one (God), three (Peter, James, and John), 12 (disciples), 120 (prayer warriors), and 5,000 (larger community).

You can't beat your porn habit on your own. And you need more than a therapist. You need a group. I suggest joining SA (Sexaholics Anonymous), SAA (Sex Addicts Anonymous), or CR (Celebrate Recovery).

Three Lessons

1. The opposite of addiction is not sobriety; it's community.

2. You can't beat your porn habit on your own.

3. Isolation is the enemy of recovery.

Today's Exercise

1. Find a group in your area. Here are a few resources.

    a. Sexaholics Anonymous: sa.org

    b. Sex Addicts Anonymous: saa-recovery.org

    c. Celebrate Recovery: celebraterecovery.com

2. After you have looked up meetings in your area, go to one. Give it at least six weeks. Write down the first meeting you will attend:

    a. Name of group: _____

    b. Date I will attend: _____

Day 18
A Daily Circle

Numbers 20:12 *"The Lord said to Moses, 'Because you did not trust in me enough to honor me as holy in the sight of the Israelites, you will not bring this community into the land I give them.'"*

One slip can bring an avalanche of trouble. Consider the case of Moses. In Numbers 20, we read the story.

Moses had just buried his sister, Miriam. The area was dry and the Israelites were desperate for water. God told Moses that he would provide a miracle, but it was critical that Moses obey his specific command.

God told Moses to take his staff in his hand and then speak to a designated rock. Water would come forth. Instead, Moses took his staff and struck the rock. Water still poured out, but his disobedience would cost Moses the opportunity to lead his people into the Promised Land.

Here's the truth we must all understand – *until God is Lord of all, he is not Lord at all*. You must give him everything.

Evangelist Dwight L. Moody often utilized the following exercise when challenging listeners to take the next step in their spiritual development. He advised them to get alone on their knees, draw a circle around themselves, and then get everyone in that circle right with God.

Most guys justify their porn habit by minimizing it. "It was just one time." "It's not hurting anybody." But one sin is like one spot of cancer. It only takes one.

Four Lessons

1. One slip can bring an avalanche of trouble.

2. Until God is Lord of all, he is not Lord at all.

3. Most guys justify their porn habit by minimizing it.

4. One sin is like one spot of cancer. It only takes one.

Today's Exercise

One slip can be devastating. One flaw can be debilitating. One bad habit, one toxic relationship, one act of disobedience – that's all it takes. Practice the Moody exercise today. Take a few minutes and get on your knees. Draw an imaginary circle around yourself. Confess every sin, every slip, every shortcoming. Confess your absolute need for Christ to be the Lord of your life. Get everyone in that circle right with God. Do it now.

Day 19

The 3-Second Rule

Job 31:1 *"I made a covenant with my eyes to not look lustfully at a young woman."*

There was a man in the Bible named Job. He experienced incredible highs and devastating lows. Through it all, he maintained his commitment to purity. To that end, Job put a plan in place to confront temptation when it came. The plan was simple. Job made an agreement with his eyes, that they would not be allowed to look at a young woman with lust.

According to one study, the average person takes in 15,000 visual images each day. Many of them are sexual in nature. And we don't have to go searching for these images. They find us.

On average, a boy's first view of pornography comes by the age of 11. And it escalates from there. But recovery is not just about not acting out. It is about progressive victory over lust. To realize that victory, we need to learn this truth – lust writes checks it cannot cash. It never fulfills.

Presbyterian theologian Frederick Buechner said it like this: "Lust is the craving for salt of a man who is dying of thirst."

Lust starts with the eyes. Visual images lodge in our minds like nothing else. The best way to win the battle is to not take in the images in the first place. And that means making a covenant with our eyes.

Four Lessons

1. Lust writes checks it cannot cash.

2. We don't have to search for sexual images; they find us.

3. You need to make an agreement with your eyes.

4. Lust begins with the eyes, but it doesn't end there.

Today's Exercise

1. Are you ready to make a covenant with your eyes? Then fill in the blanks: On this date, _____, I will commit to not look lustfully at a young woman.

2. Apply the 3-second rule. Here's how it works. Whenever you see an attractive woman, count to three. And by the time you get to three, look away. This is similar to "bouncing the eyes." But it is more specific. Chances are very good that you will have several temptations today and that you will be confronted with the kind of images that have elicited lust in the past. You may even be tempted to view pornography today or tonight. But first, apply the 3-second rule.

Day 20
Triggers

Nehemiah 4:17-18 *"Those who carried materials did their work with one hand and held a weapon in the other, and each of the builders wore his sword at his side as he worked."*

The Book of Nehemiah is a template for getting things done. Nehemiah was called by God to rebuild the wall around the holy city of Jerusalem. But it wasn't long before he encountered two men intent on stopping the work: Sanballat and Tobiah, who rallied the forces from Ammon and Ashdod to come against the children of God. The threat to Nehemiah and his work was real.

Nehemiah had to make a decision. Would he stop the work and focus on his enemies? Or would he stay on the job and ignore those who were plotting his destruction?

Nehemiah decided the answer was not either/or, but both/ and. He instructed his men to build the wall, while remaining diligent. They literally had a hammer in one hand and a sword in the other.

That is how we must walk the road of recovery. We need to move on with the project of rebuilding our lives. But at the same time, we need to keep an eye on the enemy.

You have a Sanballat or Tobiah in your life. They are called triggers. They represent any person, place, or predicament which tempt you to relapse into your old ways. You will never secure long-term sobriety until you learn how to respond to each trigger.

Two Lessons

1. You need to rebuild your life with a hammer in one hand and a sword in the other.

2. You need to identify your triggers and develop a plan to respond to each one.

Today's Exercise

1. There is a simple formula for our most common triggers. It is called H.A.L.T. These letters stand for four triggers that are a threat to each of us. We tend to act out or view porn when we are hungry, angry, lonely, or tired. Check the ones that are common triggers in your life:

   a. Hungry _____
   b. Angry _____
   c. Lonely _____
   d. Tired _____

2. Now let's get more specific. You have triggers that are unique to you and that are a serious threat to your recovery. Identify them according to the following categories:

   a. People: _____

   _____

   b. Places: _____

   _____

   c. Predicaments: _____

   _____

Day 21

Build a Wall

2 Chronicles 32:5 *"Hezekiah worked hard repairing all the broken sections of the wall and building towers on it. He built another wall outside that one and reinforced the terraces of the City of David."*

King Hezekiah understood his first responsibility – protect his people from attack. And Sennacherib posed a real threat of attack. Hezekiah had to decide. He could (a) ignore the threat, (b) prepare for the threat, or (c) go the extra mile in building his defense.

Note, Hezekiah had done nothing to deserve this. He had served God faithfully (32:1). But the king knew he had to own the problem. He went the extra mile in preparing his defense. This included three steps.

Step 1 – Hezekiah consulted with others. Specifically, "he consulted with his officials and military staff" (32:3). Similarly, when we fight for our sobriety, we must include the counsel of others: therapists, 12-step members, our sponsor, etc.

Step 2 – The king repaired what was broken. "He worked hard repairing all the broken sections of the wall" (32:5). For each of us, there are areas of our current recovery plan that generally need to be shored up.

Step 3 – Hezekiah built a second wall of defense. "He built another wall outside the first wall and reinforced it" (32:5). The final piece of the puzzle is to build a second wall of defense. This means going the extra mile to protect your sobriety.

Four Lessons

1. Sometimes, your sobriety will be threatened even when you have done nothing wrong.

2. You need to seek the counsel of others as you seek to stay pure.

3. You probably have areas of defense that need to be strengthened.

4. Going all in for your recovery means building a wall of defense, followed by a second wall of defense.

Today's Exercise

You probably already have a wall of defense which is serving you well. This might include being on Covenant Eyes (more on that later), attending SA groups, working with a sponsor, or implementing any of the exercises of the first 20 days of this program. But eventually, the enemy finds weaknesses in our walls of defense. The temptations come from all sides, and before you know it, you find yourself vulnerable to the attack.

Your job today is to brainstorm. Think of one "extra wall of defense" you can build. What can you do to secure your sobriety that you are not doing already? _____

_____

_____

_____

_____

Day 22

The 20-Minute Miracle

Genesis 3:6 *"When the woman saw that the fruit of the tree was good for food and pleasing to the eye, and also desirable for gaining wisdom, she took some and ate it. She also gave some to her husband, who was with her, and he ate it."*

When the temptation hits, it hits hard. But it doesn't last long. The story of Adam and Eve is your story and mine. In a period of just a few minutes, the first couple regressed from the purest of marriages and holiest of spiritual walks into selling out to the enemy.

The serpent was "more crafty" than any other (3:1). His process of temptation has not changed through the millennia of time: (a) insert doubt, (b) offer immediate pleasure, (c) tempt the eyes, (d) give some of the forbidden fruit.

Don't miss that last point. Eve ate "some" of the fruit, then Adam ate "some" of the fruit (3:6). This would leave them wanting more. And soon, even that which they had eaten would "wear off." They would become hungry again – soon.

When you fall to your porn temptation, the same process plays out: (a) doubt, (b) hope for a quick "fix," (c) temptation of the eyes, and (d) partaking of the forbidden.

There's good news. Just as with the temptation of Adam and Eve, it happens pretty fast. It only took a few minutes for the tempter to lure Eve (and Adam) into their version of acting out. That's how it is with porn. The urge hits, but it doesn't last. And that leads us to today's exercise.

Three Lessons

1. The temptation hits hard, but it doesn't last long.

2. Porn gives "some" pleasure, but it does not last and it does not fulfill.

3. The pleasure of the forbidden fruit leaves us coming back for more sooner than we ever expect.

Today's Exercise

It's time to learn the 20-minute rule. Physiology tells us that the sexual urge generally passes in about 20 minutes. The next time you are tempted to watch porn and masturbate, think of it like this. After about 20 minutes, the urge will have passed, for one of two reasons – you acted out, or you stayed strong and waited for it to pass.

So in about 20 minutes, the urge will likely be gone. And you will be in one of two places:

1. Grief and shame
2. Victory

The good news is that you get to decide – every time. Just remember, the next time you are tempted to view pornography or to act out in any other way, the urge will pass in about 20 minutes. Your job is to stay busy for 20 minutes doing something healthy. Then celebrate the victory.

Day 23

Go Cashless

Mark 10:21-22 *"Jesus looked at him and loved him. 'One thing you lack,' he said. 'Go, sell everything you have and give to the poor, and you will have treasure in heaven. Then come, follow me.' At this the man's face fell. He went away sad, because he had great wealth."*

Today's reading gives us the only account of a man who met with Jesus, only to walk away sad.

Here's the story. The man known as the rich, young ruler came to Jesus in search of eternal life. After a discussion of six of the ten commandments, Jesus got to the crux of the man's problem – money.

What Jesus said to the young man 2,000 years ago, he is still repeating today. "One thing you lack" (10:21). That's where most of us get into trouble. You are probably a good guy. If you are married, you may be a good husband. But like the rich, young ruler, you have this "one thing."

One thing is enough.

Let's return to this man's specific issue. He had money. Actually, his money had him. And he just didn't want to let go of it.

Do you have money that you are holding onto? Is there some hidden cash? If so, this will be your undoing, your "one thing." It may cost you your marriage, your family, your job, and your reputation. Jesus is looking right at you. "One thing you lack," he says.

The next move is yours.

Three Lessons

1. Most of us get into trouble over "one thing."

2. Until we let go completely we can't heal successfully.

3. Hidden cash makes true intimacy within your marriage impossible.

Today's Exercise

1. You need to come clean. List the financial resources that you have hidden from your spouse or others:

    a. _____

    b. _____

    c. _____

    d. _____

    e. _____

2. Are you willing to go cashless? Are you willing to quit carrying much cash in order to avoid illicit temptations?

    a. Yes _____

    b. No _____

Day 24

Mousetraps

Genesis 25:27-34 *"The boys grew up, and Esau became a skillful hunter, while Jacob was content to stay at home. Once, when Jacob was cooking some stew, Esau came in from the open country, famished. He said to Jacob, 'Quick, let me have some stew!' Jacob replied, 'First, sell me your birthright.' So Esau swore an oath to Jacob, selling him his birthright. Then Jacob gave Esau some bread and some stew. He ate and drank, then got up and left."*

In the moment, Esau gave up what he treasured most in order to capture what he wanted that second.

As the firstborn, Esau was entitled to a greater inheritance than his brother when their father died. But he let his fleshly desires get the best of him. Rather than wait a few minutes to get something else to eat, he did something insane. He gave up a lifetime of blessings (full inheritance) for the pleasure of the moment.

What did Esau get out of the deal? He got a great meal, which satisfied him for a few hours.

Sound familiar?

There's an old proverb that says, "Free cheese is always available in the mousetrap." The key to staying sexually *pure* is to avoid that which is sexually *impure*. Block the channel. Delete the phone number. Change the route. End the relationship.

There is really no limit to the number of "mousetraps" that have been set for the sex addict. In every trap is a slightly different kind of cheese. Some are more appealing than others. But they all serve their purpose.

Three Lessons

1. Free cheese is always available in the mousetrap.

2. The "free" meal only satisfies for a few hours.

3. To stay sexually pure you must avoid that which is sexually impure.

Today's Exercise

1. List the "cheese" that you are most susceptible to:
    a. _____
    b. _____
    c. _____

2. List three ways you will avoid the mousetrap.
    a. _____
    b. _____
    c. _____

Day 25
Your Devices

2 Chronicles 17:5-6 *"The Lord established the kingdom under his control; and all Judah brought gifts to Jehoshaphat, so that he had great wealth and honor. His heart was devoted to the ways of the Lord; furthermore, he removed the high places and the Asherah poles from Judah."*

Jehoshaphat became the king of the Southern Kingdom. The first thing he did was to station troops to protect the cities. And then he focused on his role as a spiritual leader.

Notice the impure influences he blocked from his life: (a) leaders of Baal, (b) high places, (c) Asherah poles. These all represented impure challenges to the sanctity of Jehoshaphat's faith, and that of his people.

What does this have to do with pornography? Everything. When a person seeks to distance himself from his porn habit, he will quickly throw out any hard copy porn. He may then delete certain social media contacts. But there is one last line of defense.

His cell phone.

The best way to know if your spouse is still acting out is to watch the way he protects or releases his phone. If he guards it like the Hope diamond, that means there is something there he doesn't want to be seen.

If you really want to overcome your porn habit – I mean if you *really* want to – you need to do something about your phone. I recommend you sign up for Covenant Eyes. For about $10 per month, you can have premier accountability. A report will be sent from Covenant Eyes to your designated accountability partner, detailing any improper use of your phone. You have to protect your devices if you want to get well.

Three Lessons

1. The best way to know if your spouse is still acting out is to watch what he does with his phone.

2. If you are no longer viewing porn or acting out in any other way, you will want your spouse to have access to your phone.

3. Until you know what your husband is doing on his phone, you don't really know your husband.

Today's Exercise

Get on Covenant Eyes. When you go to sign up, you will need to list an accountability partner and give his or her email address. Then, Covenant Eyes will send this person a weekly report which will detail any inappropriate sites you have visited on your computer or phone. A word of caution – do not list your spouse as your accountability partner. It should be someone in your 12-step group or another trusted and willing friend.

Day 26
Accountability

Ecclesiastes 4:9-10 *"Two are better than one, because they have a good return for their labor; if either of them falls down, one can help the other up. But pity anyone who falls and has no one to help them up."*

Solomon was a wise man. Raised in the home of a king, he would become a great leader of men himself. He knew a lot about relationships. His words ring true when he contemplates, "Two are better than one" (4:9).

Accountability is a bedrock of recovery. Stephen Covey wrote, "Accountability breeds response-ability." Business expert Robert Dilenschneider writes, "There are five core values that shape every good business: integrity, accountability, diligence, perseverance, and discipline."

There's that word, *accountability*, again.

In 12-step groups there are two kinds of members: those with a sponsor and those with no sponsor. As a veteran of hundreds of meetings, I have observed one irrefutable fact. Those with a sponsor go much further in their recovery than those who have no sponsor.

Lack of accountability got you in the mess you're in. If you are to overcome your porn habit, you'll need help. When you struggle to maintain your footing, you'll need someone to walk beside you, to encourage you when you do well and to challenge you when you start to fall.

Four Lessons

1. The only thing harder than maintaining sexual integrity with the support of others is to do it on your own.

2. Your spouse is not waiting for you to make new promises. She is waiting for you to keep the ones you've already made.

3. You will not become responsible until you become accountable.

4. We don't do what others *expect*; we do what they *inspect*.

Today's Exercise

1. List three places where you might find accountability.

   a. _____

   b. _____

   c. _____

2. List three people you will consider asking to be your accountability partner.

   a. _____

   b. _____

   c. _____

Day 27

The Comparison Trap

Luke 15:28-30 *"The older brother became angry and refused to go in. So his father went out and pleaded with him. But he answered his father, 'Look! All these years I've been slaving for you and never disobeyed your orders. Yet you never gave me even a young goat so I could celebrate with my friends. But when this son of yours who has squandered your property with prostitutes comes home, you kill the fatted calf for him!'"*

The story of the prodigal son is really the story of two prodigal sons. But only one of them actually left home.

When the younger brother came home, their father reacted with a wild celebration. And everyone there rejoiced - except one. The older brother fell into the comparison trap. Though his brother's return cost him nothing, and though he would still receive his inheritance as planned, he was bitter because for just a moment, someone else had stolen the spotlight.

The brother's position was pretty clear. He was the better son, so he should reap *all* the accolades.

It's easy to fall into the comparison trap on the road to recovery. When we attend an SA meeting and everyone checks in, we hear that the person sitting next to us has a more recent sobriety date than ours. And we actually rejoice in the comparison.

That's a bad idea. Your recovery is about you - no one else. All comparisons lead you to one of two conclusions: pride or low self-esteem. Both are bad.

Two Lessons

1. All comparisons lead you to one of two conclusions: pride or low self-esteem. Both are bad.

2. Your recovery is measured by your success, no one else's.

Today's Exercise

1. Say a short prayer: "God, I recognize that I'm not all I want to be. And I'm not all I'm going to be. But I'm not what I used to be, either. For that I give you thanks."

2. The only comparison you should make is to the person you want to become. List a few achievements and improvements you want to see in your recovery over the next few weeks:

    a. _____

    b. _____

    c. _____

    d. _____

    e. _____

Day 28
Guardrails

Ezekiel 33:7 *"I have made you a watchman for the people of Israel; so hear the word I speak and give them warning from me."*

Matthew Henry describes the role of the watchman in Ezekiel. He is "to discover the approaches and advances of the enemy, and to give notice to them immediately by the sound of a trumpet." God gave the role of "watchman" to his prophet. Why? Because his children need to be watched.

The goal is for us to stay on track. It's what Andy Stanley calls "driving between the guardrails." And if you are to be successful in your fight against porn, you must learn to stay inside the guardrails.

Andy points out that the smart driver doesn't drive as close to the rail as possible; he tries to stay as far away as he can. The same is true of successful recovery. You need to avoid the guardrails.

Have you heard of the "Modesto Manifesto"? Here's the story. In 1948, Billy Graham held a series of meetings in Modesto, California. His team of Cliff Barrows, Grady Wilson, and George Beverly Shea agreed to "avoid any situation that would have even the appearance of compromise or suspicion." Among other things, this meant that none of them would ever be alone with a woman other than his wife.

The lesson of the "Modesto Manifesto" is not that we should not do anything inappropriate. The lesson is that we should not even put ourselves in the position to do something inappropriate.

And that is the lesson of the guardrails.

Three Lessons

1. If you are to enjoy successful recovery, you have to learn to drive inside the guardrails.

2. You should stay as far on the other side of the road from the guardrails as you can.

3. Your goal should not be to simply avoid bad behavior, but to avoid the opportunity for bad behavior.

Today's Exercise

Write down several guardrails you are willing to put in place in order to avoid driving off course with your recovery.

1. _____

2. _____

3. _____

4. _____

5. _____

Day 29
Three Circles

Judges 16:17 *"Samson said to Delilah, 'A razor has never come upon my head, for I have been a Nazarite to God from my mother's womb. If my head is shaved, then my strength will leave me, and I shall become weak and be like any other man.'"*

This is one of the great tragedies of the Old Testament – the story of Samson and Delilah. She was able to get Samson to reveal the source of his strength, and this would cost him everything.

Under normal circumstances, Samson would not have revealed his secret. But Delilah was not normal circumstances. She had a power over him that made this giant of a man melt in her presence.

Today's exercise will involve what is known as "the three circles." In each circle, you will write a set of behaviors. The outer circle behaviors are healthy behaviors: things that help keep us sober.

Middle circle behaviors lead us into trouble. And inner circle behaviors are those which cross the line; they cost us our sobriety.

Each of us is susceptible to falling. The key is that we live in our outer circle. Samson failed to do that. He slipped into his middle circle (Delilah), which precipitated his fall.

The key to beating a porn addiction is to take the proper steps necessary to put ourselves in position to be victorious before the temptation hits. It's about being in the right place and hanging with the right crowd.

Three Lessons

1. Recovery is about being in the right place and hanging with the right crowd.

2. You need a battle plan before the battle.

3. You must define your three circles and then live by them.

Today's Exercise

1. Make a list of healthy, "outer circle" behaviors.

    a. _____

    b. _____

    c. _____

2. Make a list of "middle circle" behaviors which can lead you into trouble.

    a. _____

    b. _____

    c. _____

3. Make a list of "inner circle" behaviors – those things you can do which break your sobriety.

    a. _____

    b. _____

    c. _____

Day 30
Life's #1 Question

2 Chronicles 1:7, 10 *"That night God appeared to Solomon and said to him, 'Ask for whatever you want me to give you.' Solomon answered, 'Give me wisdom and knowledge, that I may lead this people.'"*

God always equips his children for the work that is before them. So when Solomon ascended to the throne of Israel, he was granted one wish. Of course, God knew what Solomon would ask for before the request was even made.

"Give me wisdom," Solomon answered. And God was happy to oblige.

Andy Stanley wrote a book a few years ago, titled *The Best Question Ever*. Stanley says that the best question we can ever ask is this: "What is the wise thing to do?"

You have battled pornography. This may be the toughest foe you will ever face. Will you be successful? I suggest that will come down to making wise decisions - one day at a time.

We don't fail for lack of knowledge, but lack of follow through. You generally know the right thing to do. But when you don't know, there's an answer for that. "If any of you lack wisdom, let him ask of God" (James 1:5).

Try answering your next temptation with life's #1 question. When you are within a few seconds of crossing the line, of acting out, ask yourself in the moment, "What is the wise thing to do?"

Then do it.

Four Lessons

1. You won't fail for lack of knowledge, but for lack of follow through.

2. The best question ever is this: What is the wise thing to do?

3. If you lack wisdom, ask for wisdom from God.

4. Repeat this question every time you are tempted to view porn.

Today's Exercise

It's simple. Memorize life's most important question: "What is the wise thing to do?" Then use this tool every time you are tempted to view pornography or to act out in any other way. Practice this in your thought life, as well. Before you think it or do it, put "it" to the wisdom test. Ask God for the wisdom to know the right thing to do each time – then do it!

Day 31

Find a Mentor

2 Kings 2:9 *"When they had crossed, Elijah said to Elisha, 'Tell me, what can I do for you before I am taken from you?' Elisha replied, 'Let me inherit a double portion of your spirit.'"*

The year was 1919. A young man, recovering from World War I injuries, rented a small apartment in Chicago. He chose the location so he could be close to an author named Sherwood Anderson. An aspiring author himself, the young man wanted to spend as much time with Anderson as he could. For months, they talked daily. Anderson taught his mentee everything he knew about writing.

The name of the young man was Ernest Hemingway.

There once lived an old prophet named Elijah. He did some pretty remarkable things in his career. But the time had come for a new man to replace him – a fellow named Elisha. Elisha wanted the blessing, power, and experience of his mentor. That hope was fulfilled. "The company of the prophets from Jericho, who were watching, said, 'The spirit of Elijah is now resting upon Elisha'" (2:15).

In recovery, you need someone to mentor you. This person needs to be someone who is ahead of you in recovery. He needs to have the time to answer your questions and guide you through the steps of recovery.

What you need is a sponsor.

Five Lessons

1. Only one in ten thousand finds recovery on his own.

2. You need the wisdom and experience of someone who is ahead of you in his recovery.

3. Twelve-step programs provide sponsors, who help others who are early in their sobriety.

4. It is never too soon to get a sponsor. And it is never too late.

5. You need to look for a sponsor this week.

Today's Exercise

1. Put yourself in position to find a sponsor. That requires attending at least one (preferably two) 12-step meeting per week. This may be CR, SA, or SAA. Depending on where you live, you may also find a Castimonia meeting or some other Christ-centered group. While you can always find a phone meeting (to accommodate your schedule), you need to attend a live group in order to find a sponsor.

2. Write the names of three men (women if you are female) you have already met in a group you think may be someone you could consider as a sponsor.

   a. _____

   b. _____

   c. _____

Day 32

One Day at a Time

Matthew 26:31-35 *"Then Jesus said to them, 'This very night you will all fall away on account of me. But after I have risen, I will go ahead of you into Galilee.' Peter replied, 'Even if all fall away on account of you, I never will.' 'Truly I tell you,' Jesus answered, 'this very night, before the rooster crows, you will disown me three times.' But Peter declared, 'Even if I have to die with you, I will never disown you.' And all the other disciples said the same."*

We've all said it. And we meant it. "I'll never do this again." We tell our spouse, "I'm so sorry. But I'm done. I'll never do this again."

And then it happens. We do it again.

The cycle is predictable. You've repeated it countless times: (a) you are tempted, (b) you fixate on the temptation, (c) you act out, (d) you feel remorse, (e) you promise to never do it again, and (f) you do it again.

How do you stop? One way you stop is by making a commitment to no longer make *that* commitment. I quit saying it years ago. I never promise anyone, "I won't ever act out again." Instead, I make this promise, every day – "It won't happen today."

The disciple who made the loudest pronouncement made the loudest denial – within a matter of minutes. Peter swore he'd never deny Jesus. And then he did.

You can't win tomorrow's battle today. And you can't win today's battle by looking back. The best way to have a better future is to stop trying to have a better past. Don't live in the past or the future. Live for today. That's where you find recovery – one day at a time.

Four Lessons

1. You can only find recovery one day at a time.

2. The person who pronounces his sobriety loudest usually falls hardest.

3. You can't win tomorrow's battle today.

4. The best way to have a better future is to stop trying to have a better past.

Today's Exercise

1. Repeat this: "It won't happen today." Make this a daily habit. Quit promising to never view porn again. Tell God, yourself, and your loved ones, "It won't happen today."

2. In your next 12-step meeting, collect the most important chip. It's called the "24-hour desire chip." It represents a commitment to stay sober – one day at a time.

Day 33
The Devil's Workshop

2 Samuel 11:1 *"In the spring, at the time when kings go off to war, David sent Joab out with the king's men and the whole Israelite army. They destroyed the Ammonites and besieged Rabbah. But David remained in Jerusalem."*

King David committed adultery, then set up the woman's husband to be killed on the battlefield. But before he got into trouble with Bathsheba, David got into trouble with himself. At a time when kings went off to lead their men in war, David chose to hang back in his man cave.

It was just another night at the palace, and boredom set in. Remember, David had no accountability, for he had sent his inner circle off to war. And David's couch made no demands. His "To Do" list could be done by someone else. He had servants for that.

While doing nothing, an alluring image caught his eye. Before he knew what was happening, David was captivated by the figure of a woman across the way – bathing. And then it was over.

David got into trouble because he didn't get into anything else. Bored, he became curious. Curious, he became enticed. Enticed, he became trapped – inside his own head. It all started because David was bored.

Anne Baxter said, "Idleness is a constant sin, and labor is a duty. Idleness is the devil's home for temptation and for unprofitable, distracting musings; while labor profits others and ourselves."

In one corner we have King David, the most powerful man on earth. In the other corner we have Boredom. David never had a chance.

Three Lessons

1. Before David got into trouble with Bathsheba, he got into trouble with himself.

2. The couch makes no demands.

3. David got into trouble because he didn't get into anything else.

Today's Exercise

You need to get busy. Sometimes recovery is just about doing the small stuff, the healthy stuff. It's about being involved in things that you enjoy. So take a minute and write out five projects, hobbies, or activities in which you will engage in order to stay busy and healthy.

1. _____
2. _____
3. _____
4. _____
5. _____

Day 34

Twelve-Step Groups

Luke 6:12-13 *"One of those days Jesus went out to a mountainside to pray, and spent the night praying to God. When morning came, he called his disciples to him and chose twelve of them, whom he also designated apostles."*

Jesus understood the power of a small group. He would spend more time with his 12 disciples than with the 5,000. He would share 35 parables with them, while preaching just one sermon to the masses.

We see three things here. First, Jesus was intentional about spending time with these 12 men. Second, Jesus was sure to keep this group the same sex. And third, Jesus came to rely on these men in ways he never trusted in anyone else.

For the person with a porn habit, there is something powerful about joining a 12-step group. If you resist going to meetings, I'll respond in two ways. First, I was there myself. I know how hard it is to walk into a meeting for the first time. But I did it. Praise God, I did it! And I'm still doing it, twice every week.

Second, I'll respond to your reluctance to attend SA or CR with a question – How's your current plan working for you? If you could have found sobriety on your own, you probably wouldn't be reading this right now. You need encouragement. You need accountability. What you need is a group.

Three Lessons

1. Jesus was intentional about spending time with 12 men.

2. Some attend 12-step groups, but still don't find recovery. But few find recovery without attending 12-step groups.

3. If you could have found sobriety on your own, you probably wouldn't be reading this right now.

Today's Exercise

1. We've talked about it for 34 days. Now it's time to do something about it. If you aren't already in a group, find one this week.

2. Write the name of the group and the date you will attend your first meeting: _____

Day 35
Gratitude

Mark 6:41 *"Taking the five loaves and the two fish and looking up to heaven, he gave thanks and broke the loaves. Then he gave them to his disciples to distribute to the people. He also divided the two fish among them all."*

You can read the story of the feeding of the five thousand in all four Gospels. But in all four accounts you will find something missing. At no point did Jesus pray for the Father to multiply the loaves and fish. He never actually prayed for enough food to feed the masses.

So what did he do? "Looking up to heaven, he gave thanks" (6:41). Say what? You read that correctly. Jesus took what little he had - five loaves and two fish - and offered thanks. Surely, among such a large crowd, there had been more food available earlier in the day - a snack or sandwich already eaten by now.

But here's what Jesus did. He focused on what he had left rather than on what he had lost. And then he offered thanks. The miracle was in the thanks.

It would be easy to focus on your pain, problems, and past. But you will never move forward by looking back. Instead, practice an attitude of gratitude.

Let me quote that great philosopher, Willie Nelson. He said, "When I started counting my blessings, my whole life turned around."

Do what Willie did. More importantly, do what Jesus did. Count your blessings. Offer thanks. Then enjoy the miracle.

Two Lessons

1. Focus on what you have left instead of what you have lost.

2. You will never move forward by looking back.

Today's Exercise

1. Primary blessings – write the five things for which you are the most thankful.

    a. _____
    b. _____
    c. _____
    d. _____
    e. _____

2. Secondary blessings – write ten other things for which you are thankful.

    a. _____
    b. _____
    c. _____
    d. _____
    e. _____
    f. _____
    g. _____
    h. _____
    i. _____
    j. _____

3. Stop and pray – offer thanks to God right now, for everything on both lists.

Day 36

The 'M' Question

Matthew 5:27 *"You have heard that it was said, 'You shall not commit adultery.' But I tell you that anyone who looks at a woman lustfully has already committed adultery with her in his heart."*

If your goal is absolute purity, you must confront the 'M' question – *Is it okay to masturbate?*

While this space does not allow for an extended presentation on the subject, I will offer four observations.

First, sex is a desire, not a need. In SA fellowships, all masturbation is considered out of bounds for this reason. The thinking is that any sexual outlet outside of marriage leads down a slippery slope.

Second, masturbation is generally associated with lust and fantasy. As we read in today's Scripture, lust equals adultery. Masturbation is almost always connected to porn or euphoric recall. Both are forms of lust.

Third, masturbation becomes a substitute for "the real thing." Many spouses complain that their mate has sex with himself more than with them.

Fourth, ultimately, you must decide whether masturbation is acceptable within your context. The decision should be made carefully, with prayer, and in consultation with your therapist, sponsor, and more importantly – your wife.

Five Lessons

1. God has led millions of men to stop masturbation. But he has never told one to start.

2. Sex is a desire, not a need.

3. Masturbation leads down a slippery slope.

4. Masturbation is associated with lust and fantasy.

5. Masturbation is a substitute for "the real thing."

Today's Exercise

1. You cannot move forward in your recovery until you settle the 'M' issue. Having prayed about it and sought wise counsel, it's time to nail it down. Will you commit to a life free of masturbation?
    a. Yes _____
    b. No _____

2. Write down your sobriety date, the last time you viewed porn or masturbated: _____

Day 37

Help Someone Else

Mark 2:3-4 *"Some men came, bringing to him a paralyzed man, carried by four of them. Since they could not get him to Jesus because of the crowd, they made an opening in the roof above Jesus by digging through it and then lowered the mat the man was lying on."*

Over 1,900 years before Bill W. and Bob Smith founded AA and established the 12 steps, four men practiced Step 12. Their friend was hopelessly lame, and they knew his best chance of healing was to get him to Jesus. But when they got to the home Jesus was visiting, they quickly realized the place was too full; there was no room to enter through the door.

There was such an urgency about their desire to get the man help that they didn't even wait for the crowd to disperse, when they could have caught Jesus on his way out. So they carved a hole in the roof and lowered their friend down before the Great Physician.

Your recovery will not be complete until you help someone else. Winston Churchill said it like this: "We make a living by what we get. We make a life by what we give."

It may seem crazy that you can help others while still struggling yourself. But think back to the four men who lowered their friend down to Jesus. They all had their own issues; we all do. But imagine the joy they must have felt when they helped someone else on the road to healing.

Three Lessons

1. The best way to get someone in recovery is to take them to Jesus.

2. We make a living by what we get; we make a life by what we give.

3. You don't find recovery and *then help others*; you find recovery *by helping others*.

Today's Exercise

1. List the names of three friends who need to be in recovery or who need to go further in their recovery.

   a. _____

   b. _____

   c. _____

2. Write out a plan to help someone in need of recovery. Be specific.

Day 38
Travel Plan

Daniel 1:5, 8 *"The king assigned them a daily amount of food and wine from the king's table. They were to be trained for three years, and after that they were to enter the king's service. But Daniel resolved not to defile himself with the royal food and wine, and he asked the chief official for permission not to defile himself this way."*

Daniel was taken captive by Nebuchadnezzar, king of Babylon. Along with his friends, he was offered the finest that the foreign land – home of false gods – had to offer. All he had to do was play along.

"But Daniel resolved not to defile himself" (1:8). For as long as he would be in this foreign land, Daniel was committed to the God of his homeland.

Recovery is a matter of establishing new routines and habits. That means establishing consistency. But sometimes we have to travel, and this puts our sobriety at risk. And that is when we must be the most diligent.

Paul said, "Let he who thinks he stands be careful, lest he fall" (1 Corinthians 10:12). We must never take a single day of sobriety for granted. We must have a plan in place whenever we leave home.

Two Lessons

1. Recovery is a matter of establishing routine.

2. Sometimes we have to travel, and this puts our sobriety at risk.

Today's Exercise

1. These are the things you need to do before you leave home.
   a. Get a list of meetings in the area where you will be.
   b. If you can't attend a live meeting, get the contact information for phone-in meetings.
   c. Write a daily recovery plan for your trip.
   d. Tell your sponsor when you will be gone.
   e. Make sure you have several members' cell numbers from your home group.
   f. Make sure your spouse knows your schedule.

2. These are the things you need to do while you are away from home.
   a. Attend at least one 12-step meeting per week.
   b. Call your sponsor each week.
   c. Call two members of your home group each day.
   d. Tell your spouse where you are at all times.
   e. Avoid past areas where you might have acted out.
   f. Avoid former acting out partners.
   g. Read daily recovery material.
   h. Read from your Life Recovery Bible every day.

Day 39

Recovery Day

Matthew 26:36 *"Then Jesus went with them to a place called Gethsemane, and he said to his disciples, 'Sit here, while I go over there and pray.'"*

Jesus knew his time was near. After a period of ministry and with the cross just ahead, he got away one last time. We notice three things about that special night.

First, we notice the timing. Jesus had experienced great success. His ministry on earth was nearly complete. He had successfully healed, preached, and laid the foundation on which the church would be built for the next two thousand years and beyond. But now he faced the cross. So on the heels of amazing success and on the precipice of his darkest hour, Jesus got away.

Second, we notice what Jesus did. He prayed. His focus was spiritual. Jesus was intentional about his relationship with the Father. He wasn't about to enter the final phase of his life without that spiritual connection being strong.

Third, we notice that Jesus took others with him, but then went on ahead by himself. We need others in our lives. But there are times when we need to just get away with our Father.

Our focus today is on establishing a Recovery Day. This is a day to replicate what Jesus did so long ago. It is a time to refuel, recharge, and remember.

Let's get started.

Three Lessons

1. On the heels of great success or on the precipice of our darkest hour, we need a Recovery Day.

2. Jesus wasn't about to enter the final phase of his life without his spiritual connection being strong.

3. We need others in our lives. But there are times when we need to just get away with our Father.

Today's Exercise

1. Set aside a date for your first Recovery Day. If possible, set aside an entire day: _____

2. The following are the things you might include in your Recovery Day. Check off each one you will try to include, plus anything else you think might be beneficial to your personal recovery.
   a. Place to be alone with God outdoors _____
   b. SA, SAA, CR meeting to attend _____
   c. Literature to read _____
   d. Journaling _____
   e. Extended time of prayer _____
   f. One fun activity _____
   g. Call to sponsor or friend _____
   h. Bible reading _____
   i. Other _____

Day 40

Spiritual Awakening

Ezekiel 37:1-2, 17 *"The hand of the Lord was on me, and he brought me out by the Spirit of the Lord and set me in the middle of a valley; it was full of bones . . . bones that were very dry . . . The Lord said, 'I will put my Spirit in you and you will live, and I will settle you in your own land. Then you will know that I the Lord have spoken, and I have done it, declares the Lord.'"*

God brought his prophet Ezekiel to the valley of dry bones. Then we read one of the great stories of the Old Testament. God promised these dry bones would come to life again. It was all about a spiritual awakening – an awakening that would give hope to God's children.

Philosopher Teilhard de Chardin was right: "We are not human beings having a spiritual experience. We are spiritual beings having a human experience."

Consider the parable of the saw. A man had a firewood factory that employed hundreds of men. He paid them to cut the wood to certain specifications. But their work was slow. Eventually, the owner of the factory fired all the men and replaced them with a circular saw powered by a gas engine. He now got more done in a day than the crew could do with their old-fashioned saws in a month.

The man asked his new saw, "How can you turn out so much work? Are you sharper than the saws my men were using before?"

"No," said the saw. "I'm more productive because of the power that is flowing through me."

You need a Power flowing through you. You need a spiritual connection.

Three Lessons

1. You need a spiritual connection.

2. You are not a physical being having a spiritual experience; you are a spiritual being having a physical experience.

3. You can start recovery on your own, but you can only finish it with the help of God.

Today's Exercise

1. Are you committed to a spiritual connection?
   a. Yes _____
   b. No _____

2. Things you are willing to do to maintain a spiritual connection:
   a. Daily Scripture reading _____
   b. Daily prayer time _____
   c. Weekly worship _____
   d. Regular times of meditation _____
   e. Christian fellowship _____
   f. Confession of personal sin _____
   g. Daily surrender to God _____

ABOUT THE AUTHOR

Mark and Beth Denison are the founders and directors of "There's Still Hope," a Christ-centered sex addiction recovery ministry. With a comprehensive focus on addicts, spouses, and pastors, TSH provides multi-faceted resources: personal coaching, group work, one-day intensives, 90-day recovery plans, a one-year maintenance plan, daily online devotions, and other printed materials.

For 30 years, Mark served as a senior pastor to three different churches in his home state of Texas. He also served on the Board of Trustees for his alma mater (three times as chair), Houston Baptist University. For five seasons, Mark served as a chaplain to the Houston Rockets. He has earned four degrees, including a D.Min. and M.Div. from Southwestern Baptist Theological Seminary, and a Master's Degree in Addiction Recovery from Liberty University. Mark is also an active member of the American Association of Christian Counselors.

Mark and Beth are proud parents of one son, who is also involved in ministry. They live near the beaches of Bradenton, Florida, and serve in leadership at their local church.

Mark has published four other books: *The Daily Walk, Porn in the Pew, 365 Days to Sexual Integrity,* and *90-Day Recovery Guide.*

For more information on There's Still Hope, visit their website at TheresStillHope.org.

www.ingramcontent.com/pod-product-compliance
Lightning Source LLC
LaVergne TN
LVHW051151080426
835508LV00021B/2575